CW01476888

Bath
Travel Guide

Quick Trips Series

No part of this publication may be reproduced, stored in a retrieval system, or transmitted, in any form or by any means without the prior written permission of the publisher, nor be otherwise circulated in any form of binding or cover other than that in which it is published and without similar condition being imposed on the subsequent purchaser. If there are any errors or omissions in copyright acknowledgements the publisher will be pleased to insert the appropriate acknowledgement in any subsequent printing of this publication. Although we have taken all reasonable care in researching this book we make no warranty about the accuracy or completeness of its content and disclaim all liability arising from its use.

Copyright © 2016, Astute Press
All Rights Reserved.

Table of Contents

Bath

Bath is a famous Roman/Georgian spa city that is located 95 miles west of London and 20 miles southeast of Bristol. The city is located in the lovely Somerset countryside to the south of the Cotswolds. Bath is a UNESCO World Heritage Site, known for its ancient hot springs, Roman baths, impressive architecture and medieval heritage.

BATH TRAVEL GUIDE

Bath has a population of 85,000 and offers much to its four million annual visitors: restaurants, theatres, cinemas, pubs and nightclubs, along with interesting museums, and a wide range of guided tours.

For hundreds of years, visitors came to Bath to bathe in its natural spa waters. It was believed that the water had healing properties and would cure diseases from arthritis to infertility. Bath remains a highly visited location in the United Kingdom today, for somewhat different reasons.

Around 60 AD, the Romans built *Aquae Sulis*, the 'spa' that would later become Bath. Hot springs attracted them to the area, where they built temples and baths for the next 300 or more years. Fortifications were constructed to provide security to the high level lords and officers that wanted to use the location to relax.

BATH TRAVEL GUIDE

The original temples and buildings were all built out of wood and sod and because of this the spring eventually caved in upon itself, drying the town's prosperity for a little while. In the sixth century, the town then fell into the hands of the Anglo-Saxons as the Roman Empire slowly began to draw back towards Rome. At first the city prospered, but as it had with the Romans, it was not long before Bath fell into ruins.

King Alfred rebuilt the town of Bath in the middle of the ninth century, and the town once again became influential. Bath Abbey was even used for the crowning ceremony of King Edgar in 973. Unfortunately, for the next six hundred years, Bath continued to fall in and out of repair as influence shifted amongst nobleman and their favored lands.

BATH TRAVEL GUIDE

It was not until Queen Elizabeth I granted Bath city status in 1590 that the town began to keep more up to date with the times and stop its cycles into disrepair. After this time, the wealthiest of English citizens would travel to Bath to take in the water, hoping that the Romans were right and there was healing properties to the water. If they did not go for the baths themselves, the city was a bustling place to catch up with society's top tiers, bringing more people to Bath as higher-ranking nobles visited.

By 1801, Bath was one of the largest cities in England. Unfortunately, its location in the east and away from a seaport kept it from staying up with the populations of larger cities like London or Manchester, so it slowly lost its influence as more industrialized areas of Britain gained popularity.

BATH TRAVEL GUIDE

During World War II, however, the Nazis destroyed the historical landmark of Bath during the Bath Blitz. On April 25, 1942, nearly 400 people were killed in the city, and many landmarks were destroyed or damaged, although most have been completely rebuilt since.

Today, Bath is a major UK tourist attraction. People like to visit Bath because it is still possible to see the majestic architecture that has spanned two millennia. You can still see the effects on the city of the English Civil War and World War II. It is a great place to visit no matter which era of history you enjoy best.

To search an online map of Bath visit:

http://visitbath.co.uk/travel-and-maps/bath-city-centre-map

🌐 Customs & Culture

The history of Bath spans millennia and has a unique culture influenced by each of its previous occupants. Today, Bath has many different events that are focused on preserving the influences brought by each of these cultures. Bath is a city focused on the arts. Music festivals, such as the Bath International Music Festival and Mozartfest, bring in many visitors each year. Bath also holds annual beer, film, literature, and art festivals. Besides once being considered the place to go to be healed by its waters, Bath has also been considered as one of the most fashionable places in England outside of London. Bath has a typical British culture with lots of heated discussions about football, reality TV shows and the royal family.

🌐 Geography

Bath is located in Southwest England in the county of Somerset. Bath is built in the Avon River Valley on the Lansdown Plateau 156 km west of London, and about 21 km southeast of Bristol. Because it is only two hours away from London, and many other large cities in England, Bath is very popular for those seeking a day or weekend trip.

There are a number of different ways to get to Bath. If flying, the closest airport is in Bristol (BRS). From Bristol, it is just a short drive to Bath. For a cheaper flight, you can also choose to land at any of the London airports and either drive or take a train to Bath. The Bath Spa Railway Station has connections to many of the larger cities, like London, Bristol, Cardiff, Plymouth, and more. There are also numerous buses available to many towns and cities.

Driving to Bath is simple as it is just off of M4 or M5 depending on the direction you are travelling from. However parking can be tricky and there are few places that you can park for free.

🌍 Weather & Best Time to Visit

Choosing when to visit Bath depends largely on the weather and whether or not you want to attend any of Bath's popular festivals. Given its location, Bath is typically wetter and cooler than much of the rest of the United Kingdom. For summer months, this means an average temperature of about 21°C (70°F). In the winter, the temperature drops to around 1°C (33.8°F).

There are usually only 8 to 15 days of snow each year. There is plenty of rainfall with Bath getting about 700 mm each year.

BATH TRAVEL GUIDE

Easter marks the beginning of festival season in Bath. March brings the Bath Literature Festival. April Fools Day marks the start of the Bath Comedy Festival and May Day is the opening of the annual flower show at the Royal Victoria Park. Even if festivals are not your thing, spring is a good season to visit Bath and there are not as many tourists as there are in the summer.

Once summer begins, Bath is full of visitors soaking up as much sun as possible. The summer festivals center on music. No matter when you decide to visit Bath, it is quieter to visit during the week. Typically, Bath is considered a one-day trip by those who live close by, so it can be busy during the weekend. During the week, tourists tend to those from outside of the region who are on holiday.

Sights & Activities: What to See & Do

🌏 Parade Gardens

Orange Grove

Bath, England BA1 1EE

Tel: 44-1225-477101

http://visitbath.co.uk/things-to-do/attractions/parade-

gardens-p25551

Located near Pulteney Bridge and Bath Abbey, the

Parade Gardens offer a great pause from all of the museums, ruins, and shopping that Bath has to offer. After paying a £1 fee, guests can enjoy the lovely Parade Gardens.

There are many different places to just sit down and relax, along with a café to give the opportunity to snack during your downtime. The botanical gardens inside the Parade Gardens offer guests a view of many different plants that they may not otherwise have the opportunity to see.

Herschel Museum of Astronomy

19 New King Street

Bath, England BA1 2LB

Tel: 44 01225 446865

http://herschelmuseum.org.uk

BATH TRAVEL GUIDE

Hours: Weekdays 1300-1700; Weekends 1100-1700

Adult: £6; Student: £3.50; Concession: £5.50; Children: £3

Built in 1764, the Herschel Museum of Astronomy was once the home of William Herschel, the famed British astronomer. It was in this house that he built many of his telescopes and other inventions. It was here that Herschel discovered Uranus in March 1781. In 1981, the house was purchased and restored to the original Georgian style. Today, it is one of the many museums in Bath that are run by the Bath Preservation Trust.

In the Herschel Museum of Astronomy, guests can view many of Herschel's homemade telescopes, his Star Vault, and even see his workshop where he spent many hours creating tools to take a closer look at the sky. There are also exhibits dedicated to Herschel's sister, Caroline, who followed in her brother's footsteps and became the first female astronomer, making many discoveries of her own over the years.

Holburne Museum of Art

Great Pulteney Street

Bath, England BA2 4DB

Tel: 44 01225 388569

www.holburne.org

Hours: Monday-Saturday 1000 to 1700; Sundays and Bank Holidays 1100 to 1700

The Holburne Museum of Art celebrates art collector Sir Thomas William Holburne and the large selection of art he amassed during his time as a Baron. His collection drew to include items such as silver, Chinese armorial porcelain, Italian maiolica, portrait miniatures, paintings, books, furniture, gems, seals, snuff boxes, and much more. In total, Holburne acquired over 4,000 items in his lifetime. In 1893, a museum was opened to celebrate the art that he left behind after his death.

In 1916, the Holburne Museum of Art moved to the Sydney Hotel, where it resides today. Guests not only get the opportunity to view the art collection that now holds nearly 7,000 items, but also get to walk around the historic Bath hotel, which was built in 1796. The museum also includes a café, giving guests the opportunity to grab some food before the heading off to their next stop.

🌐 Royal Victoria Park

Marlborough Lane (Across from the Royal Crescent)

Bath, England BA1 2NQ

BATH TRAVEL GUIDE

Tel: 44 01225 394041

http://visitbath.co.uk/things-to-do/attractions/royal-victoria-park-p25701

The Grand Royal Victoria Park is located near the center of Bath. The fifty-seven acre area was created in honor of Princess Victoria, and it was the first location in England to have her namesake. Unlike your normal, run-of-the-mill park, the Royal Victoria Park has many different things to offer. There are numerous walking trails, statues, and monuments. The botanical gardens within the park are a must stop for all. Guests can also enjoy boating pond, a golf course, a bird aviary, a skate park, tennis courts, a bowling green, and a children play area. During the summer, the Royal Victoria Park is also a popular venue to attend outdoor concerts, which run nearly every weekend. Admittance into the park itself is free, but some

of the extras within the park compound may charge a fee.

🌎 American Museum

Claverton Manor

Bath, England BA2 7BD

Tel: 44 1225 460503

<u>www.americanmuseum.org</u>

Adults: £10; Concession: £9; Children: £5.50

Hours: March 23-November 3 (Tuesday-Sunday) 1200-

1700; November 28-December 22 (Tuesday-Sunday)

1200-1630

Without Britain, the United States of America would be

quite different today. The American Museum brings the

history of the United States to Britain. From a replica of

George Washington's garden at Mount Vernon to an

entire room dedicated to outlaws like Bonnie and Clyde, Buffalo Bill and Calamity Jane, many different aspects of Americana are represented in the museum. The American Museum in Bath is considered to be one of the best museums on American history outside of the county. The café serves typical 'American' foods, such as barbeque and fried chicken. They also serve things that are only found in the United States, like snickerdoodle cookies. This is a great stop for children, as the United Kingdom and the United States have such a close bond. The museum is a great place for both countries to learn about each other.

🌐 Fashion Museum & Assembly Rooms

Bennett Street

Bath, England BA1 2QH

BATH TRAVEL GUIDE

Tel: 44 01225 477789

www.museumofcostume.co.uk

Adult: £7.75/Child: £5.75/Seniors and Students: £7

Hours: Daily 1030 to 1700

The Fashion Museum (or the Museum of Costume as it was previously known) covers the fashion of Bath and England over the centuries. Besides the Dress of the Year collection that grows each year, the museum also has many different collections that focus on particular items and time periods, such as their current collection of 17th century gloves. There are also collections made by some of the fashion designers that have come from the Bath area. The collection has grown from its original, which was started by Doris Langley Moore, a resident of Bath. Today, the museum holds more than 30,000 items from the late 16th century to present day.

Besides the Fashion Museum, the building is also home to the Assembly Rooms. The building itself was opened in 1771, and was used as a place to dance, listen to music, play cards, and catch up with others from the city. Today, guests can visit the Ball Room, the Tea Room, the Octagon Room, and the Card Room. During the visit, guests can also see some of the damage that was caused by bomb raids during the Bath Blitz of World War II, although most of it has been rebuilt to its former state.

🌐 Farleigh Hungerford Museum

Norton St. Philip

Bath, England BA2 7RS

www.english-heritage.org.uk/daysout/properties/farleigh-hungerford-castle/

Adult: £4.10/Children: £2.50/Concession: £3.70

BATH TRAVEL GUIDE

Hours: March 29-September 30: Daily 1000-1800;

October 1-November 3: Daily 1000-1700; November 4-

March 28: Saturday and Sunday 1000-1600

Farleigh Hungerford Castle was first built in 1377 by Sir

Thomas Hungerford and expanded upon again in 1383. It

was originally built of nothing more than wood using

riches won during the Hundred Years War. Eventually, it

was reconstructed of stone to ensure that it would last for

years. Between the 17th and 18th century, gambling debt

forced the family to sell off the castle, which then fell into

disrepair. In 1844, it first opened as a museum of

curiosities, which also focused on some of the murals that

were painted when it was first built. In 1915, English

Heritage purchased the castle, and has since worked to

restore various areas of the castle as close as possible

back to its original state.

While some of the areas in the castle have now been destroyed by centuries of inclement weather and war, there are still some areas of the castle that are open for others to walk around in and see different exhibits that have been put into place. Most of these exhibits follow the history of the castle and the area of surrounding Bath, but also include of the original items that could be found in the museum of curiosities. It is important to note that it is 12.7 km from downtown Bath, so it may not be accessible to those who do not have a car available to them.

🌐 Bath Abbey

12 Kingston Buildings

Bath, England BA1 1LT

Tel: 44 01225 422462

www.bathabbey.org

BATH TRAVEL GUIDE

Hours (main office): Monday to Friday 900-1600

The Abbey Church of Saint Peter and Saint Paul was originally founded in the 7th century. It was rebuilt on three separate occasions in the 10th, 12th, and 16th centuries and underwent its final major renovation in the 1860s. Like the city itself, the Abbey holds a lot of history. In 675 AD it was first established as a convent. By 973, it had been overhauled to become one of the grandest churches in England, and even served as the location where Edgar was crowned "King of the English." Pope Innocent IV eventually gave the Abbey cathedral status in 1245. However, like the city around it, Bath Abbey fell into disrepair. And finally, in 1574, Queen Elizabeth I helped to create a campaign to help raise the money needed to fully repair the building to its former glory.

Besides being a fully functioning church were guests can attend mass or spend time in prayer, Bath Abbey has more than 1500 memorials and stone tiles dedicated to various people from Bath and/or English history that guests are invited to look over. The Heritage Vaults Museum is also located inside Bath Abbey, which displays the long history of the current building and along with its many previous constructions.

🌐 Roman Baths Museum

18 Stall Street

Bath, England BA1 1LZ

Tel: 44 01225 477785

www.romanbaths.co.uk

Adult: £12.75/Child: £8.50/Senior and Student: £11

Hours: March-June and September-October: 900-1700;

July-August: 900-2100;

BATH TRAVEL GUIDE

November-February: 930-1630

Around 836 BC, the first baths were built near the spring in modern day Bath out of nothing more than wood and clay. When the Romans conquered the area in 60 AD, they created a structure to house the baths and keep them usable for those who passed through the city, and especially for the lords. Unfortunately, the Roman Baths were long forgotten as the city fell in and out of disrepair over the years.

Since the bronze head of the goddess Sulius Minerva was discovered in 1727, thousands of Roman artifacts have been found in the Bath area, including a pile of over 30,000 Roman coins that were underground so long that they look as though they melted together. At the Roman Baths Museum, guests get the opportunity to not only see

these amazing objects, but also see the remnants of the
baths themselves, namely the main hot springs that today
reside underground.

A visit to the Roman Baths Museum is not to be missed
on any trip to Bath where you have the opportunity to see
the history of the city beginning more than 2000 years
ago. The hot spring is also considered today to be one of
the Seven Natural Wonders, it is one of the top sites to
see.

🌑 Jane Austen Centre

40 Gay Street

Bath, England BA1 2NT

Tel: 44 01225 443000

www.janeausten.co.uk/

Adult: £8/Child: £4.50/Student: £6/Senior: £7

BATH TRAVEL GUIDE

Hours: March 24-November 3: Daily 945-1730; November 4-March 23: Daily 1100-1730

Based on the life of Bath's most famous resident, the Jane Austen Centre gives guests a view of what life was like during the author's life in the city.

Although the building was not where Austen lived, it has been renovated to fit the style of what homes in her time would have looked like, and is only a few doors down from her former home. Each room has exhibits that either cover life in Bath at the beginning of the 1800s or one of her books and other writings.

The museum workers dress to fit the time period, pulling guests further into her world. Guests also have the opportunity to dress in these different styles of clothing. The Centre also has a tea room where guests can enjoy a light snack and a gift shop where they can purchase Jane Austen themed merchandise.

🌐 Building of Bath Collection

38 The Paragon

Bath, England BA1 5NA

Tel: 44 01225 333895

www.buildingofbathcollection.org.uk

Adult: £5; Seniors and Students: £4; Child: £2.50

Hours: February 9-November 24: Tuesday-Friday 1400-1700; Saturday and Sunday 1030-1700

The Building of Bath Collection is one of the only museums in Bath that focus on how the city evolved from a tiny Roman spa into the large city that it is today.

The museum is home to artifacts spanning hundreds of years of life in the city, such as paintings, tools, and coins used by previous occupants of the city. There is also a detailed model of historic Bath so guests can see what the city looked like in the past. Even the house that the Building of Bath Collection is housed in is considered one of the treasures of Bath, built in 1765 as a Presbyterian Church.

The Circus

Intersection of Gay Street and Bennett Street

Bath, England BA1 1EE

Tel: 44 01225 477101

The Circus was built in 1754 to house social gathers and games. Master Bath Architect John Woods Sr. used the Coliseum of Rome as inspiration for his this new building.

The Circus was built as three long, curved terraces that all connect together, with architectural detail becoming grander as you go up the levels. In the center of the circle is an old garden with trees planted by some of the original tenants. Although much of the Circus remains private, it is home to a restaurant that guests can stop and enjoy the history in. Or, you can just sit in the garden and relax while taking in the sites.

🌐 Royal Crescent

1-30 Royal Crescent

Bath, England BA1 2LR

www.royalcrescentbath.com

Tel: 44 01225 477101

Following in his father's footsteps, architect John Woods Jr. built what today is considered the most spectacular terrace in Bath. Construction of the unique building began in 1767 and finished in 1774.

What makes the Royal Crescent stand out is that after Woods designed the main parts of the building, people could purchase a length of the building to build their own house with their own designs behind it, meaning that from the front, the building looks uniform, and from the back each individual building is different. Currently, many of the houses have been converted into apartments or offices. The Royal Crescent Hotel occupies Number 16 Royal Crescent, exactly in the middle of the crescent, and Number 1 Royal Crescent serves as historic house museum run by the Bath Preservation Trust. Royal Victoria Park runs directly across the street from the Royal Crescent, providing beautiful views from its many windows.

🌎 Stonehenge

Off A344 Road

Amesbury, Wiltshire, England SP4 7DE

Tel: 44 0870 3331181

http://www.english-

heritage.org.uk/daysout/properties/stonehenge/

Adult: £8/Child: £4.80/Concession: £7.20

Hours: June 1-August 31 900-1700; September 1-October

15 930-1800;

October 16-March 15 930-1600

In the middle of a field of burial mounds 56 km east of

Bath sits Stonehenge, one of the most ancient and

fascinating sites anywhere in the world.

How these large stones were placed in their circle more

than 5000 years ago has long been a mystery, which is

what makes it so popular amongst historians. This is because theories on how the stones ended up in the middle of a field standing straight up in an almost perfect circle range anywhere from them being built by ancient civilizations to them being put in place by aliens looking for a door to travel quickly to Earth.

What archaeologists have determined is that areas around the monument have evidence of people dating back about 8000 years. Around 3000 BC, construction on what would eventually become Stonehenge began with the building of a large ditch and mound. The stones that are visible today most likely come from the third stage of construction. The stones stand 4.1 meters tall and weigh approximately 25 tons. From what archaeologists can determine, Stonehenge was left incomplete (as the circle is incomplete). However, it is also possible that some of the stones were subsequently removed from the area

after they were placed in the circle.

Apart from a basic timeline of when things appeared,

there really is no knowing why Stonehenge was

constructed. There are a few carvings on the stones of

things like an arrow or animals, but they make no real

sense as to what they might mean when placed together.

It is equally uncertain as to what the purpose of

Stonehenge was. Some believe that it was a place for

healing. Others believe it is a monument to the dead who

lay in the surrounding fields. Or, to those with an active

imagination, it may have been a portal to another

dimension or another world.

Whatever theory you believe about why or how it was

built, the one thing that is certain is that a day trip to

Stonehenge is a must. Although special permission must be given to walk amongst the stones, visitors can see amazing views of the artifacts from only a short distance away. The history and mystery behind Stonehenge are compelling, and it attracts many visitors each year.

Budget Tips

🌎 Accommodation

Beds at Bath

Claverton Down

Bath, England BA2 7AY

Tel: 44 01225 386622

https://www.bath.ac.uk/hospitality/beds/

For a unique experience, Beds at Bath is a perfect place to spend the night. Instead of your normal hotel, Beds at Bath is located on the University of Bath campus inside the student residence halls. The rooms offer basic accommodations such as a TV, coffee/tea maker, and an ensuite bathroom. There is also a community lounge and full kitchen.

Because these are student residences, availability varies based on the time of year. During the school year, rooms are available for £66 per night. As more rooms become available after students leave for the summer, room prices drop to between £27 and £66 per night, although the cheapest rooms don't include private bathrooms.

Pratt's Hotel

4-8 S Parade

Bath, England BA2 4AB

Tel: 44 01225 460441

http://www.forestdalehotels.com/Hotels/Southern-England/Pratts-Hotel-Bath

Originally built as five separate town houses in 1743, Pratt's Hotel has been used as everything from a home to a boarding house for nearly 200 years. Today, the hotel provides excellent accommodations close to the city center, Bath Abbey, the Roman Baths, and reasonably priced car parks. Rooms include free Wi-Fi, TV, coffee/tea making facilities, hairdryer, and 24 hour room service. To add to its allure, Pratt's hotel also offers themed rooms and a classic Georgian restaurant. Rooms range from £90 to £125 depending on which day of the week that a guest stays.

Lansdown Grove Hotel

Lansdown Road

Bath, England BA1 5EH

Tel: 44 01225 583888

http://www.coastandcountryhotels.com/england/weston-super-mare-and-somerset/hotels/the-lansdown-grove-hotel?cm_mmc=Online-_-TripAdvisor-_-Listing-_-Default

The original building was constructed in the 1770s as a manor for a wealthy family.

In the mid 1800s, it was converted to a hotel, and is considered one of the oldest in Bath. Today's hotel combines old world charm with all of the modern amenities guests are looking for. Rooms come with a television, Wi-Fi, hairdryer, tea/coffee making facilities, and en-suite bathrooms. The hotel also offers its own car park, a patio, a garden terrace, and a bar. Rooms start out around £125 per night.

YHA Youth Hostel

Bathwick Hill

Bath, England BA2 6JZ

Tel: 0845 3719303

http://www.yha.org.uk/hostel/bath

A youth hostel can be a great place to stay. YHA Bath is a modern hostel with excellent facilities. The Italian-style mansion is set within its own private gardens. There is Wi-Fi, community bathrooms, laundry facilities, and a self-service kitchen. Another unique aspect of YHA Bath is that it is home to a full restaurant. Shared rooms cost £26 per person, while private rooms start out at £28 per person. Breakfast is available for £5.

Oldfield's House

102 Wells Road

Bath, England BA2 3AL

Tel: 44 01225 317984

www.oldfields.co.uk

Only a ten minute walk from the city center, Oldfield's

House is an elegant hotel for a decent price. The old style Victorian house upholds classical elegance while providing guests with all of the modern amenities they are looking for. The hotel provides guests with Wi-Fi, air conditioning, a DVD library, and free parking, a rarity in Bath. Some rooms also offer guests a Jacuzzi in their room, along with full breakfast included in the rate. Oldfield's House offers a large variety of rooms, ranging in price from £85 to £190.

Redcar Hotel

27-29 Henrietta Street

Bath, England BA2 6LR

Tel: 44 01225 469151

www.redcarhotelbath.co.uk

Located next to Pulteney Bridge, Redcar Hotel offers a warm, welcoming place to stay right in the heart of Bath.

The hotel was converted from three Georgian town houses in 1949 from buildings that were first constructed in 1788. The hotel has 40 rooms available, each of which comes with a television, telephone, hair dryer, toiletries, and tea and coffee making facilities. Redcar Hotel is also home to the Chandos Bar & Lounge, which has a wide range of spirits, wines and beers for sale. Parking is free on weekdays, but it costs £10 on Friday and Saturday due to its location in the center of town. Rooms range from £45 to £110.

Wentworth House Hotel

106 Bloomfield Road

Bath, England BA2 2AP

Tel: 44 01225 339193

www.wentworthhouse.co.uk

Located near to the Roman Baths and Bath Abbey, Wentworth House is a former estate that has been transformed to a twenty room hotel complete with a restaurant, an English garden, a bar and lounge, and an outdoor swimming pool. Guest parking is free, useful in Bath. They also offer dry cleaning and laundry, coffee and tea making facilities, Wi-Fi and hair dryers. Room prices begin at £65 and go up depending on the type of room that is booked.

Restaurants, Cafés & Bars

Best of British Deli

12 Broad Street

Bath, England BA1 5LJ

Tel: 44 01225 448055

www.bestofbritishdeli.co.uk

This 100% organic deli and café offers traditional British food made the traditional way. Its specialty is gourmet sandwiches and quiches, and anything that is not made by them is made by other local companies. Do not let the 'gourmet' claim rule out the deli because of price, as all sandwiches are all reasonably priced.

Roman Baths Kitchen

11-12 Abbey Churchyard

Bath, England BA1 1LY

Tel: 44 01225 477877

http://searcys.co.uk/venues/roman-baths-kitchen/#.Ug5mgJLUkTk

The location of The Roman Baths Kitchen next to Bath Abbey and the Pump Room coupled with its well-priced meals make it a great spot to relax and catch a bite to eat. The Roman Baths Kitchen is separated into two parts, with the ground floor being a café and the upstairs being a bistro style restaurant.

Marlborough Tavern

35 Marlborough Buildings

Bath, England BA1 2LY

Tel: 44 01225 423731

http://www.marlborough-tavern.com/index.php

For an award winning pub experience, the Marlborough Tavern is the place to stop. Located just behind the Royal Crescent, it makes the perfect place to stop for a pint and some food after a long day seeing the many sights of

Bath. Menus change daily, so guests can expect a wide variety of dishes any day that they visit. The homemade British cuisine is made with locally grown items.

Demuth's Vegetarian Restaurant

2 North Parade Passage

Bath, England BA1 1NX

Tel: 44 01225 446059

http://www.demuths.co.uk/about/introduction/

Demuth's Vegetarian Restaurant is Bath's only 100% vegetarian restaurant. Located just next to the Bath Abbey, it offers a full seven course meal, or guests can choose meals a la carte. Guests can expect only the best locally grown fresh produce. They also offer menu items that are vegan and wheat and gluten free. If you want to learn more about vegetarian cooking, the owner, Rachel Demuth, also offers cooking classes that highlight some of her most popular dishes.

Bath Bun Tea Shoppe

2 Abbey Green

Bath, England BA1 1NW

Tel: 44 01225 463928

http://www.thebathbun.com/

Around 1761, the Bath Bun, a sweet roll with plenty of sugar accompanying it, first made its appearance and soon became a local delicacy. The Bath Bun Tea Shoppe has been the 'home' of the Bath Bun since they were created. Dr. William Oliver created the Bath Bun to help treat rheumatism. But, as you will see as soon as you try one of these delicious cakes, they soon became popular to the public and were considered to be responsible for

the fattening of Bath society. At the restaurant, guests can

purchase a variety of drinks, pastries, and sandwiches, all

of which make a great afternoon tea.

Seafood's Traditional Fish & Chips

38 Kingsmead Street

Bath, England BA1 2AA

Tel: 44 01225 465190

http://seafoodsfishandchips.co.uk/

Fish & Chips has been a staple of the English diet for

years.

While on your visit to Bath, be sure to enjoy this British

meal at Seafood's Traditional Fish & Chips, who have

been serving it for nearly 80 years. All food is made to

order, which means you will be eating nothing but the

freshest foods. Unlike many other shops that specialize in

Fish & Chips, Seafood's allows you to dine in, and has a

private dining room for up to 50 people. It is also

conveniently located in the center of Bath, very near many

of Bath's monuments.

Central Bar

10 Upper Borough Walls

Bath, England BA1 1RG

Tel: 44 01225 333939

http://centralbarbath.co.uk/

Located downtown near all of the main attractions,

Central Bar offers modern bar life in an 18th century

locale. Central Bar offers everything from soup to

sandwiches, trout, or roast. They also have a full

breakfast menu and larger plates of food as well. And, of

course, they have everything from specialty cocktails to

champagne.

🌍 Shopping

Milsom Place

Milsom Street & Broad Street

Bath, England BA1 1BZ

Tel: 44 01225 789040

www.milsomplace.co.uk

Milsom Place is one of Bath's most popular shopping

centers and was converted from Gregorian style

buildings. From food, to shopping, to special events,

Milsom Place has a little bit of everything for everyone.

There are nearly 30 shops and restaurants in the

complex, many of them small shops that are locally owned and operated. Although the shops are small, do not confuse this with a lack of up to date fashion, which is what Milsom Place is most known for.

SouthGate Bath

12 Southgate Street

Bath, England BA1 1AQ

Tel: 44 01225 469061

www.southgatebath.com

Bath's newest shopping center, SouthGate Bath, is also one of its largest.

With over 55 shops, there are a wide variety of products that suit everyone. Top shops from around the world are represented at SouthGate Bath, like H&M, Hollister,

Tommy Hilfiger, The North Face, Topshop, and many more. If shopping the world's top fashions is not your style, perhaps a break at any of the centers restaurants will make a great stop, with both fast food and sit-down style options available.

Bartlett Street Antique Center

5-10 Bartlett Street

Bath, England BA1 2QZ

Tel: 44 01225 466689

In a city with as much history as Bath, a trip to one of its best antique malls is a necessity. The Bartlett Street Antique Center is a great place to buy smaller antiques, perfect for taking home on after your visit to Bath. The center is full of stalls of antique dealers ready to sell you your own piece of history. Bags, jewelry, weapons, and more are all available for purchase at the centers more than 60 stands. Bartlett Street Antique Center is the perfect location to buy gifts for your loved ones that will mean much more to them than that magnet with photos of Bath on it.

Pulteney Bridge

9-10 Pulteney Bridge

Bath, England BA2 4AY

Tel: 44 01225 446097

Built in 1774, Pulteney Bridge is a unique bridge that crosses the Avon River. It is one of only four bridges in the world that have shopping available on both sides of the bridge the entire span of the river. Although Pulteney Bridge has been rebuilt and remodeled over the years, it still holds its original charm and architecture. This makes it not only a great spot to shop but also a great

sightseeing location. Sit in any of the cafés that are also

located on the Pulteney Bridge and watch the boats travel

back and forth underneath where you are sitting while you

relax.

The Corridor

19 High Street

Bath, England BA1 5AP

http://www.thecorridorbath.co.uk/

The Corridor is the oldest shopping center in Bath, and

also one of the oldest in the world. It originally opened on

October 12, 1825, and has seen many famous

shopkeepers come and go over nearly two centuries. The

shopping center is relatively small, with about 25 units.

However, the old world charm coupled with the great

shops make it well worth a visit. Its central location also

makes it a great stopping point after a visit to Bath Abbey

or the Royal Crescent.

🌐 Entry Requirements

Citizens of the European Union do not need a visa when visiting the UK. Non-EU members from European countries within the European Economic Area (EEA) are also exempt. This includes countries like Iceland, Norway, Liechtenstein and Switzerland. Visitors from Canada, Australia, Japan, Malaysia, Hong Kong SAR, New Zealand, Singapore, South Korea and the USA do not need a visa to visit the UK, provided that their stay does not exceed 6 months. Visitors from Oman, Qatar and the United Arab Emirates may apply for an Electronic Visa Waiver (EVW) via the internet, if their stay in the UK is less than 6 months. You will need a visa to visit the UK, if travelling from India, Jamaica, Cuba, South Africa, Thailand, the People's Republic of China, Saudi Arabia, Zimbabwe, Indonesia, Cambodia, Nigeria, Ghana, Kenya, Egypt, Ethiopia, Vietnam, Turkey, Taiwan, Pakistan, Russia, the Philippines, Iran, Afghanistan and more. If you are in doubt about the status of your country, do inquire with officials of the relevant UK Embassy, who should be able to advise you. Visitors from the EU (European Union) or EEA (European Economic Area) will not require immigration clearance when staying in the Isle of Man, but may require a work permit if they wish to take employment there. If needed, a visa for the Isle of Man may be obtained from the British Embassy or High Commission in your country. Applications can be made via the Internet.

If you wish to study in the UK, you will need to qualify for a student visa. There are a number of requirements. First, you have to provide proof of acceptance into an academic institution and available funding for tuition, as well as monthly living costs. A health surcharge of £150 will be levied for access to the National Health Service. Applications can be made online and will be subject to a points based evaluation system.

If you need to visit the UK for professional reasons, there are several different classes of temporary work visas. Charity volunteers, sports professionals and creative individuals can qualify for a stay of up to 12 months, on submission of a certificate of sponsorship. Nationals from Canada, Australia, Japan, Monaco, New Zealand, Hong Kong, Taiwan and the Republic of Korea can also apply for the Youth Mobility Scheme that will allow them to work in the UK for up to two years, if they are between the ages of 18 and 30. Citizens of Commonwealth member countries may qualify for an ancestral visa that will enable them to stay for up to 5 years and apply for an extension.

Health Insurance

Visitors from the European Union or EEA (European Economic Area) countries are covered for using the UK's National Health Service, by virtue of a European Health Insurance Card (EHIC). This includes visitors from Switzerland, Liechtenstein, the Canary Islands and Iceland. The card can be applied for free of charge. If you are in doubt about the process, the European Commission has created phone apps for Android, IPhone and Windows to inform European travellers about health matters in various different countries.

Bear in mind that a slightly different agreement is in place for Crown Dependencies, such as the Isle of Man and the Channel Islands. There is a reciprocal agreement between the UK and the Isle of Man with regards to basic healthcare, but this does not include the option of repatriation, which could involve a considerable expense, should facilities such as an Air Ambulance be required. If visiting the UK from the Isle of Man, do check the extent of your health insurance before your departure. A similar reciprocal agreement exists between the UK and the Channel Islands. This covers basic emergency healthcare, but it is recommended that you inquire about travel health insurance if visiting the UK from the Channel Islands.

BATH TRAVEL GUIDE

The UK has a reciprocal healthcare agreement with several countries including Australia, New Zealand, Barbados, Gibraltar, the Channel Islands, Montserrat, Romania, Turkey, Switzerland, the British Virgin Islands, the Caicos Islands, Bulgaria, the Falkland Islands and Anguilla, which means that nationals of these countries are covered when visiting the UK. In some cases, only emergency care is exempted from charges. Reciprocal agreements with Armenia, Azerbaijan, Belarus, Georgia, Kazakhstan, Kyrgyzstan, Moldova, Russia, Tajikistan, Turkmenistan, Ukraine and Uzbekistan were terminated at the beginning of 2016 and no longer apply.

Visitors from non European countries without medical insurance will be charged 150 percent of the usual rate, should they need to make use of the National Health Service (NHS). Exemptions exist for a number of categories, including refugees, asylum seekers. Anyone with a British work permit is also covered for health care. Find out the extent of your health cover before leaving home and make arrangements for adequate travel insurance, if you need additional cover.

Travelling with pets

If travelling from another country within the EU, your pet will be able to enter the UK without quarantine, provided that certain entry requirements are met. The animal will need to be microchipped and up to date on rabies vaccinations. This means that the vaccinations should have occurred no later than 21 days before your date of departure. In the case of dogs, treatment against tapeworm must also be undertaken before your departure. You will need to carry an EU pet passport. If travelling from outside the EU, a third-country official veterinary certificate will need to be issued within 10 days of your planned departure. Check with your vet or the UK embassy in your country about specific restrictions or requirements for travel with pets.

In the case of cats travelling from Australia, a statement will need to be issued by the Australian Department of Agriculture to confirm that your pet has not been in contact with carriers of the Hendra virus. If travelling from Malaysia, you will need to carry documentation from a vet that your pet has tested negative for the Nipah virus within 10 days before your departure. There are no restrictions on pet rodents, rabbits, birds, reptilians, fish, amphibians or reptiles, provided that they are brought from another EU country. For pet rabbits and rodents from countries outside the European Union, a four month quarantine period will be required, as well as a rabies import licence. Entry is prohibited for prairie dogs from the USA and squirrels and rodents from sub-Saharan Africa.

🌐 Airports, Airlines & Hubs

Airports

London, the capital of England and the UK's most popular tourist destination is served by no less than 6 different airports. Of these, the best known is **Heathrow International Airport (LHR)**, which ranks as the busiest airport in the UK and Europe and sixth busiest in the world. Heathrow is located about 23km to the west of the central part of London. It is utilized by more than 90 airlines and connects to 170 destinations around the world. The second busiest is **Gatwick Airport (LGW)**, which lies 5km north of Crawley and about 47km south of the central part of London. Its single runway is the world's busiest and in particular, it offers connections to the most popular European destinations. From 2013, it offered travellers a free flight connection service, called Gatwick Connect if the service is not available through their individual airlines. **London Luton Airport (LTN)** is located less than 3km from Luton and about 56km north of London's city center. It is the home of EasyJet, the UK's largest airline, but also serves as a base for Monarch, Thomson Airlines and Ryanair. **London Stansted Airport (STN)** is the fourth busiest airport in the UK. Located about 48km northeast of London, it is an important base for Ryanair and also utilized by EasyJet, Thomas Cook Airline and Thomson Airways. **London Southend Airport (SEN)** is located in Essex, about 68km from London's central business area. Once the third busiest airport in London, it still handles air traffic for EasyJet and Flybe. Although **City Airport (LCY)** is the nearest to the city center of London, its facilities are compact and limiting. The short runway means that it is not really equipped to handle large aircraft and the airport is not operational at night either. It is located in the Docklands area, about 6.4km from Canary Wharf and mainly serves business travellers. Despite these restrictions, it is still the 5th busiest airport in London and 13th busiest in Europe.

The UK's third busiest airport is **Manchester International Airport (MAN)**, which is located about 13.9km southwest of Manchester's CBD. **Birmingham Airport (BHX)** is located 10km from Birmingham's CBD and offers connections to domestic as well as international destinations. **Newcastle International Airport (NCL)** is located about 9.3km from Newcastle's city center and offers connections to Tyne and Wear, Northumberland, Cumbria, North Yorkshire and even Scotland. **Leeds/Bradford Airport (LBA)** provides connections to various cities in the Yorkshire area, including Leeds, Bradford, York and Wakefield. **Liverpool International Airport (LPL)**, also known as Liverpool John Lennon Airport, serves the north-western part of England and provides connections to destinations in Germany, France, Poland, the Netherlands, Spain, Greece, Cyprus, the USA, the Canary

Islands, Malta, Jersey and the Isle of Man. **Bristol Airport (BRS)** provides international access to the city of Bristol, as well as the counties of Somerset and Gloucestershire. As the 9th busiest airport in the UK, it also serves as a base for budget airlines such as EasyJet and Ryanair. **East Midlands Airport (EMA)** connects travellers to Nottingham.

Edinburgh Airport (EDI) is the busiest in Scotland and one of the busier airports in the UK. Its primary connections are to London, Bristol, Birmingham, Belfast, Amsterdam, Paris, Frankfurt, Dublin and Geneva. Facilities include currency exchange, a pet reception center and tourist information desk. **Glasgow International Airport (GLA)** is the second busiest airport in Scotland and one of the 10 busiest airports of the UK. As a gateway to the western part of Scotland, it also serves as a primary airport for trans-Atlantic connections to Scotland and as a base for budget airlines such as Ryanair, Flybe, EasyJet and Thomas Cook. **Cardiff Airport (CWL)** lies about 19km west of the city center of Cardiff and provides access to Cardiff, as well as the south, mid and western parts of Wales. In particular, it offers domestic connections to Glasgow, Edinburgh, Belfast, Aberdeen and Newcastle. **Belfast International Airport (BFS)** is the gateway to Northern Ireland and welcomes approximately 4 million passengers per year. **Kirkwall Airport (KOI)** was originally built for use by the RAF in 1940, but reverted to civilian aviation from 1948. It is located near the town of

Kirkwall and serves as gateway to the Orkney Islands. It is mainly utilized by the regional Flybe service and the Scottish airline, Loganair. The airports at **Guernsey (GCI)** and **Jersey (JER)** offer access to the Channel Islands.

Airlines

British Airways (BA) is the UK's flag carrier airline and was formed around 1972 from the merger of British Overseas Airways Corporation (BOAC) and British European Airways (BEA). It has the largest fleet in the UK and flies to over 160 destinations on 6 different continents. A subsidiary, BA CityFlyer, manages domestic and European connections. British Airways Limited maintains an executive service linking London to New York. The budget airline EasyJet is based at London Luton Airport. In terms of annual passenger statistics, it is Britain's largest airline and Europe's second largest airline after Ryanair. With 19 bases around Europe, it fosters strong connections with Italy, France, Germany and Spain. Thomas Cook Airlines operates as the air travel division of the Thomas Cook group, Britain and the world's oldest travel agent. Thomson Airways is the world's largest charter airline, resulting from a merger between TUI AG and First Choice Holidays. The brand operates scheduled and chartered flights connecting Ireland and the UK with Europe, Africa, Asia and North

America. Founded in the 1960s, Monarch Airlines still operates under the original brand identity and maintains bases at Leeds, Birmingham, Gatwick and Manchester. Its primary base is at London Luton Airport. Jet2.com is a budget airline based at Leeds/Bradford, which offers connections to 57 destinations. Virgin Atlantic, the 7th largest airline in the UK, operates mainly from its bases at Heathrow, Gatwick and Manchester Airport.

Flybe is a regional, domestic service which provides connections to UK destinations. Covering the Channel Islands, Flybe is in partnership with Blue Islands, an airline based on the island of Guernsey. Blue Islands offers connections from Guernsey to Jersey, London, Southampton, Bristol, Dundee, Zurich and Geneva. Loganair is a regional Scottish airline which is headquartered at Glasgow International Airport. It provides connections to various destinations in Scotland, including Aberdeen, Edinburgh, Inverness, Norwich and Dundee. Additionally it operates a service to the Shetland Islands, the Orkney Islands and the Western Islands in partnership with Flybe. BMI Regional, also known as British Midland Regional Limited, is based at East Midlands Airport and offers connections to other British destinations such as Aberdeen, Bristol and Newcastle, as well as several cities in Europe.

BATH TRAVEL GUIDE

Hubs

Heathrow Airport serves as a primary hub for British Airways. Gatwick Airport serves as a hub for British Airways and EasyJet. EasyJet is based at London Luton Airport, but also maintains a strong presence at London's Stansted Airport and Bristol Airport. Manchester Airport serves as a hub for the regional budget airline Flybe, as does Birmingham Airport. Thompson Airways maintain bases at three of London's airports, namely Gatwick, London Luton and Stansted, as well as Belfast, Birmingham, Bournemouth, Bristol, Cardiff, Doncaster/Sheffield, East Midlands, Edinburgh, Exeter, Glasgow, Leeds/Bradford, Manchester and Newcastle. Jet2.com has bases at Leeds/Bradford, Belfast, East Midlands, Edinburgh, Glasgow, Manchester and Newcastle. Glasgow International Airport serves as the primary hub for the Scottish airline, Loganair, which also has hubs at Edinburgh, Dundee, Aberdeen and Inverness.

Sea Ports

As the nearest English port to the French coast, Dover in Kent has been used to facilitate Channel crossings to the European mainland for centuries. This makes it one of the busiest passenger ports in the world. Annually, 16 million passengers,

71

2.8 million private vehicles and 2.1 million trucks pass through its terminals. Three ferry services to France are based on the Eastern dock, connecting passengers to ports in Calais and Dunkirk. Additionally, the Port of Dover also has a cruise terminal, as well as a marina.

The Port of Southampton is a famous port on the central part of the south coast of the UK. It enjoys a sheltered location thanks to the proximity of the Isle of Wight and a tidal quirk that favours its facilities for bulky freighters as well as large cruise liners. The port serves as a base for several UK cruise operators including Cunard, Celebrity Cruises, P&O Cruises, Princess Cruises and Royal Caribbean. Other tour operators using its terminals include MSC Cruises, Costa Cruises, Crystal Cruises and Fred. Olsen Cruise Lines. Southampton is a popular departure point for various cruises to European cities such as Hamburg, Rotterdam, Amsterdam, Le Havre, Bruges, Barcelona, Lisbon, Genoa and Scandinavia, as well as trans-Atlantic destinations such as Boston, New York and Miami. A short but popular excursion is the two day cruise to Guernsey. Southampton also offers ferry connections to the Isle of Wight and the village of Hythe. The port has four cruise terminals and is well-connected by rail to London and other locations in the UK.

Eurochannel

The Eurotunnel (or the Channel Tunnel) was completed in 1994 and connects Folkestone in Kent with Coquelles near Calais. This offers travellers a new option for entering the UK from the European continent. Via the Eurostar rail network, passengers travelling to or from the UK are connected with destinations across Europe, including Paris, Brussels, Frankfurt, Amsterdam and Geneva. On the UK side, it connects to the London St Pancras station. Also known as St Pancras International, this station is one of the UK's primary terminals for the Eurostar service. The Eurotunnel Shuttle conveys private and commercial vehicles through the tunnel and provides easy motorway access on either side.

🌍 Money Matters

Currency

The currency of the UK is the Pound Sterling. Notes are issued in denominations of £5, £10, £20 and £50. Coins are issued in denominations of £2, £1, 50p, 20p, 10p, 5p, 2p and 1p. Regional variants of the pound are issued in Scotland and Northern Ireland, but these are acceptable as legal tender in other parts of the UK as well. The Isles of Jersey, Guernsey and

Man issue their own currency, known respectively as the Jersey Pound, the Guernsey Pound and the Manx Pound. However, the Pound Sterling (and its Scottish and Northern Irish variants) can also be used for payment on the Isle of Man, Jersey and Guernsey.

Banking/ATMs

ATM machines, also known locally as cashpoints or a hole in the wall, are well distributed in cities and larger towns across the UK. Most of these should be compatible with your own banking network, and may even be enabled to give instructions in multiple languages. A small fee is charged per transaction. Beware of helpful strangers, tampering and other scams at ATM machines. Banking hours vary according to bank group and location, but you can generally expect trading hours between 9.30am and 4.30pm.

Credit Cards

Credit cards are widely accepted at many businesses in the UK, but you may run into smaller shops, restaurants and pubs that do not offer credit card facilities. Cash is still king in the British pub, although most have adapted to credit card use. For hotel bookings or car rentals, credit cards are essential. Visa and MasterCard are most commonly used. Acceptance of American Express and Diners Club is less widespread. Chip and PIN cards are the norm in the UK. While shops will generally have card facilities that can still accept older magnetic strip or US chip-and-signature cards, you will find that ticket machines and self service vendors are not configured for those types of credit cards.

Tourist Tax

A tourist tax of £1 for London has been under discussion, but to date nothing has been implemented. The areas of Cornwall, Brighton, Edinburgh, Westminster and Birmingham also considered implementing a tourist tax, but eventually rejected the idea.

Claiming back VAT

If you are not from the European Union, you can claim back VAT (or Value Added Tax) paid on your purchases in the UK. The VAT rate in the UK is 20 percent, but to qualify for a refund, certain conditions will have to be met. Firstly, VAT can only be claimed merchants participating in a VAT refund program scheme. If this is indicated, you can ask the retailer for a VAT 407 form. You may need to provide proof of eligibility by producing your passport. Customs authorities at your point of departure from the European Union (this could be the UK or another country) will inspect the completed form as well as your purchased goods. You should receive your refund from a refund booth at the airport or from the refund department of the retailer where you bought the goods.

Tipping Policy

It is customary to tip for taxis, restaurants and in bars where you are served by waiting staff, rather than bartenders. The usual rate is between 10 and 15 percent. Some restaurants will add this automatically to your bill as a service charge, usually at a rate of 12.5 percent. Tipping is not expected in most pubs, although you may offer a small sum (traditionally the price of a half pint), with the words "and have one yourself". Some hotels will also add a service charge of between 10 and 15 percent to your bill. You may leave a tip for room-cleaning staff upon departure. Tip bellboys and porters to express your gratitude for a particular service, such as helping with your luggage or organizing a taxi or booking a tour. Tipping is not expected at fast food, self service or takeaway outlets, but if the food is delivered, do tip the delivery person. You may also tip a tour guide between £2 and £5 per person, or £1 to £2 if part of a family group, especially if the person was attentive, engaging and knowledgeable. In Scotland, most restaurants do not levy a service charge and it is customary to tip between 10 and 15 percent. Tipping in Scottish pubs is not necessary, unless you were served a meal.

🌐 Connectivity

Mobile Phones

Like most EU countries, the UK uses the GSM mobile service. This means that visitors from the EU should have no problem using their mobile phones, when visiting the UK. If visiting from the USA, Canada, Japan, India, Brazil or South Korea, you should check with your service provider about compatibility and roaming fees. The US service providers Sprint, Verizon and U.S. Cellular employ the CDMA network, which is not compatible with the UK's phone networks. Even if your phone does use the GSM service, you will still incur extra costs, if using your phone in the UK. For European visitors the rates will vary from 28p per minute for voice calls and 58p per megabyte for data. The alternative option would be to purchase a UK sim card to use during your stay in the UK. It is relatively easy to get a SIM card, though. No proof of identification or address details will be required and the SIM card itself is often free, when combined with a top-up package.

The UK has four mobile networks. They are Vodafone, O2, Three (3) and EE (Everything Everywhere), the latter of which grew from a merger between Orange and T-Mobile. All of these do offer pay-as-you-go packages that are tailor made for visitors. Through EE, you will enjoy access to a fast and efficient 4G network, as well as 3G and 2G coverage. There is a whole range of pay as you go products, which are still part of the Orange brand. These have been named after different animals, each with a different set of rewards. The dolphin package, which includes free internet and free texts will seem ideal to most tech savvy travellers. The canary plan offers free calls, texts and photo messages, while the raccoon offers the lowest call rate. Also through EE, you can choose from three different package deals, starting from as little as £1 and choose whether to favour data or call time.

With the Three packages, you will get a free SIM with the All-in-One package of £10. Your rewards will include a mix of 500Mb data, 3000 texts and 100 minutes calltime. It is valid for 30 days. Through the O2 network, you can get a free SIM card, when you choose from a selection of different top-up packages, priced from £10. As a service provider, O2 also offers users an international SIM card, which will enable you to call and text landline as well as mobile numbers in over 200 countries. With Vodafone, you can choose between a mixed top-up package that adds the reward of data to the benefit of voice calls and data only SIM card offer. The packages start at £10.

Alternately, you could also explore the various offers from a range of virtual suppliers, which include Virgin Mobile, Lebara Mobile, Lycamobile, Post Office Mobile and Vectone Mobile. Virtual Packages are also available through the retailers Tesco and ASDA.

Dialling Code

The international dialling code for the UK is +44.

Emergency Numbers

General Emergency: 999
(The European Union General emergency number of 112 can also be accessed in the UK. Calls will be answered by 999 operators)
National Health Service (NHS): 111
Police (non-emergency): 101

MasterCard: 0800 056 0572

Visa: 0800 015 0401

🌎 General Information

Public Holidays

1 January: New Year's Day (if New Year's Day falls on a Saturday or Sunday, the 2nd or 3rd of January may also be declared a public holiday).

17 March: St Patrick's Day (Northern Ireland only)

March/April: Good Friday

March/April: Easter Monday

First Monday in May: May Day Bank Holiday

Last Monday in May: Spring Bank Holiday

12 July: Battle of the Boyne/Orangemen's Day (North Ireland only)

First Monday of August: Summer Bank Holiday (Scotland only)

Last Monday of August: Summer Bank Holiday (everywhere in the UK, except Scotland)

30 November: St Andrew's Day (Scotland only)

25 December: Christmas Day

26 December: Boxing Day

(if Christmas Day or Boxing Day falls on a Saturday or Sunday, 27 and/or 28 December may also be declared a public holiday)

Time Zone

The UK falls in the Western European Time Zone. This can be calculated as Greenwich Mean Time/Co-ordinated Universal Time (GMT/UTC) 0 in winter and +1 in summer for British Summer Time.

Daylight Savings Time

Clocks are set forward one hour at 01.00am on the last Sunday of March and set back one hour at 02.00am on the last Sunday of October for Daylight Savings Time.

School Holidays

In the UK, school holidays are determined by city or regional authorities. This means that it could vary from town to town, but general guidelines are followed. There are short breaks to coincide with Christmas and Easter, as well as short mid terms for winter (in February), summer (around June) and autumn (in

October). A longer summer holiday at the end of the academic year lasts from mid July to the end of August.

Trading Hours

For large shops, trading hours will depend on location. There are outlets for large supermarket chains such as Asda and Tesco that are open round the clock on weekdays or may trade from 6am to 11pm. In England and Wales, the regulations on Sunday trading are set according the size of the shop. While there are no restrictions on shops less than 280 square meters, shops above that size are restricted to 6 hours trading on Sundays and no trading on Christmas or Easter Sunday. Post office trading hours vary according to region and branch. Most post offices are open 7 days a week, but hours may differ according to location.

In Scotland, the trading hours for most shops are from 9am to 5pm, Monday to Saturdays. In larger towns, urban city areas and villages frequented by tourists, many shops will elect to trade on Sundays as well. Some rural shops will however close at 1am on a weekday, which would usually be Wednesday or Thursday. Some shops have introduced late trading hours on Thursdays and longer trading hours may also apply in the summer months and in the run-up to Christmas. On the Scottish islands of Lewis, Harris and North Uist, all shops will be closed on a Sunday.

Driving Policy

In the UK, driving is on the left side of the road. Both front and rear passengers must wear seat belts. If travelling with children, they must be accommodated with an age-appropriate child seat. With rental cars, it is advisable to make prior arrangements for this when you arrange your booking. If stopped by the police, you may be asked for your driver's licence, insurance certificate and MOT certificate, which must be rendered within 7 days. Driving without insurance could result in the confiscation of your vehicle.

In urban and residential areas, the speed limit for all types of vehicles is 48km per hour. On motorways and dual carriageways, cars, motorcycles and motor homes less than 3.05 tonnes are allowed to drive up to 112km per hour. On a single carriageway, this drops to 96km per hour. For motorhomes above 3.05 tonnes and vehicles towing caravans or trailers, the speed limit is 80km for single carriageways and 96km for dual carriageways and motorways. Local speed limits may vary. The alcohol limit for drivers is 35mg per 100ml of breath in England

and Wales and 22mg per 100ml of breath in Scotland (or 80mg and 50mg respectively per 100ml of blood).

Drinking Policy

The legal age for buying alcohol in the UK is 18. Young persons of 16 to 17 may drink a single beer, cider or glass of wine in a pub, provided they are in the company of an adult. From the age of 14, persons can enter a pub unaccompanied to enjoy a meal and children are allowed in pubs with their parents until 9pm. For buying alcohol at an off-license, you will need to be over 21 and may be asked to provide identification.

Smoking Policy

In the UK, smoking is prohibited in public buildings, all enclosed spaces and on public transport. Smoking is also prohibited at bus shelters. The law also states that 'no smoking' signage must be displayed clearly within all premises covered by the legislation. The only exceptions are rooms specifically designated as smoking rooms.

Electricity

Electricity: 230 volts

Frequency: 50 Hz

The UK's electricity sockets are compatible with the Type G plugs, a plug that features three rectangular pins or prongs, arranged in a triangular shape. They are incompatible with the two pronged Type C plugs commonly used on the European continent, as UK sockets are shuttered and will not open without the insertion of the third "earth" pin. If travelling from the USA, you will need a power converter or transformer to convert the voltage from 230 to 110, to avoid damage to your appliances. The latest models of certain types of camcorders, cell phones and digital cameras are dual-voltage, which means that they were manufactured with a built in converter, but you will have to check with your dealer about that.

Food & Drink

England gave the world one of its favourite breakfast, the Full English, a hearty feast of bacon eggs, sausage, fried mushroom and grilled tomato. In the UK, this signature dish is incomplete without a helping of baked beans. In Scotland, you can expect to see black pudding or Lorne sausage added to the ensemble, while the Welsh often throw in some cockles or Laverbread.

For simple, basic meals, you cannot go wrong with traditional pub fare. All round favourites include the beef pie, shepherd's pie, bangers and mash and toasted sandwiches. Fish and chips, served in a rolled up sheet of newsprint, is another firm favourite. For Sunday roast, expect an elaborate spread of roasted meat, roasted potatoes, vegetables and Yorkshire pudding. The national dish of Scotland is, of course, Haggis - sheep's offal which is seasoned and boiled in a sheep's stomach. This dish rises to prominence on Burns Night (25 January), when the birthday of the poet Robert Burns is celebrated. Burns wrote 'Address to a Haggis'. The influence of immigrants to the UK has led to kosher haggis (which is 100 percent free of pork products) and an Indian variant, Haggis pakora, said to have originated from the Sikh community. The synergy of Anglo-Indian cuisine also gave rise to popular dishes such as Chicken Tikka Masala and Kedgeree.

The neighbourhood pub is an integral part of social life in the UK and Britain is known for its dark ale, also referred to as bitter. Currently, the most popular beer in the UK is Carling, a Canadian import which has available in the British Isles since the 1980s. Foster's Lager, the second most popular beer in the UK, is brewed by Scottish & Newcastle, the largest brewery in Britain. For a highly rated local brew, raise a mug of award-winning Fuller's beer. The brewery was established early in the 1800s and produces London Pride, London Porter and Chiswick

Bitter, to name just a few. A popular brand from neighbouring Ireland is Guinness. Along with Indian curries, the market share of Indian beer brands like Jaipur or Cobra beer has grown in recent years. Kent has developed as an emergent wine producer.

On the non-alcoholic side, you can hardly beat tea for popularity. The English like to brew it strong and serve it in a warmed china teapot with generous amounts of milk. Tea is served at 11am and 4pm. Afternoon tea is often accompanied with light snacks, such as freshly baked scones or cucumber sandwiches. High tea, served a little later at 6pm, can be regarded as a meal. A mixture of sweet and savoury treats such as cakes, scones, crumpets, cheese or poached egg on toast, cold meats and pickles. The custom of High Tea goes back to the days when dinner was the midday meal. These days, it is often replaced by supper.

Scotland is known for producing some of the world's finest whiskies. Its industry goes back at least 500 years. One of Scotland's best selling single malt whisky is produced by the famous Glenmorangie distillery in the Highlands. Chivas Brothers, who once supplied whisky by royal warrant to Queen Victoria's Scottish household, produce Chivas Regal, one of the best known blended whiskies of Scotland. The Famous Grouse, which is based at Glenturret near the Highlands town of Crieff, produces several excellent examples of blended grain whiskies.

Bell's Whisky is one of the top selling whiskies in the UK and Europe. Other well known Scottish whisky brands include Old Pulteney, Glen Elgin, Tamdhu (a Speyside distillery that produces single malt), Balvenie, Bunnahabhain, Macallan, Aberlour, Bowmore, the award-winning Ballantine and Grant's whisky, from a distillery that has been run by the same family for five generations. Another proudly Scottish drink is Drambuie, the first liqueur stocked by the House of Lords. According to legend, its recipe was originally gifted to the MacKinnon clan by Bonnie Prince Charlie.

Events

Sports

Horse racing is often called the sport of kings and has enjoyed the support of the British aristocracy for centuries. Here you can expect to rub shoulders with high society and several races go back to the 1700s. The Cheltenham Festival is usually on or near St Patrick's Day and now comprises a four day event of 27 races. The Grand National takes place in Liverpool in April. With prize money of £1 million, this challenging event is Europe's richest steeplechase. A Scottish equivalent of the Grand National takes place in Ayr in the same month. There is also a Welsh Grand National, which now takes place in the winter at Chepstow. A past winner of Welsh event was none other than the author Dick Francis. Other important horse races are the Guineas at Newmarket (April/May), the Epsom Oaks and the Epsom Derby (first Saturday of June) and the St Leger Stakes, which takes place in Doncaster in September. One of the annual highlights is Royal Ascot week, traditionally attended by the British Royal Family. This takes place in June at Berkshire. There is a strict dress code and access to the Royal Enclosure is limited, especially for first timers. Fortunately, you will be able to view the the arrival of the monarch in a horse drawn carriage with a full royal procession at the start of the day. Another high profile equestrian event is the St Regis International Polo Cup, which takes place in May at Cowdray Park.

Wimbledon, one of the world's top tennis tournaments, takes place in London from last week of June, through to the first half of July. If you are a golfing enthusiast, do not miss the British Open, scheduled for July at Royal Troon in South Ayrshire, Scotland. The event, which has been played since 1860, is the world's oldest golf tournament. A highlight in motorcycle racing is the Manx Grand Prix, which usually takes place in August or September and serves as a great testing ground for future talent. The British Grand Prix takes place at Silverstone in Northamptonshire. A sporting event that occupies a special place in popular culture is the annual boat race that usually takes place in April between the university teams of Oxford and Cambridge. The tradition goes back to 1829 and draws large numbers of spectators to watch from the banks of the Thames. The FA Cup final, which is played at Wembley Stadium in May, is a must for soccer fans. As a sports event, the London Marathon is over 100 years old and draws entries from around the world to claim its prize money of a million pounds. Keen athletes will only have a brief window period of less than a week to submit their entries. Selection is by random ballot. The 42km race takes place in April.

Cultural

If you want to brush shoulders with some of your favourite authors or get the chance to pitch to a British publisher or agent, you dare not miss the London Book Fair. The event takes place in April and includes talks, panel discussions and exhibitions by a large and diverse selection of publishing role players. The London Art Fair happens in January and features discussions, tours and performances. For comic geeks there are several annual events in the UK to look forward to. The CAPTION comic convention in Oxford, which goes back to the early 1990s, is a must if you want to show your support to Britain's small presses. There is a Scottish Comic Con that takes place in the Edinburgh International Conference Center in April and a Welsh Comic Con, also in April, at Wrexham. The MCM London Comic Con happens over the last weekends of May and October, and covers anime, manga, cosplay, gaming and science fiction in general. The UK's calendar of film festivals clearly shows its cultural diversity. The oldest events are the London Film Festival (October) and the Leeds Film Festival (November). There are also large events in Manchester and Cambridge. The high-profile Encounters festival for shorts and animated films takes place each September in Bristol.

History fans can immerse themselves in the thrills and delights of the Glastonbury Medieval Fayre, which takes place in April and includes stalls, jousting and minstrels. The Tewkesbury Medieval Festival takes place in summer and its key event is the re-enactment of the Battle of Tewkesbury.

Edinburgh has an annual International Film Festival that takes place in June. The city also hosts a broader cultural festival that takes place in August. The Edinburgh International Festival is a three week event that features a packed programme of music, theatre, dance and opera, as well as talks and workshops. The Royal Highland show takes place in June and features agricultural events as well as show jumping. If you want to experience the massing of Scottish pipers, one good opportunity is the Braemar Gathering, an event that takes place on the first Saturday in September and is usually attended by the Royal family. Its roots go back 900 years. Over the spring and summer seasons, you can attend numerous Highland Games, which feature Scottish piping, as well as traditional sports such as hammer throw and tug of war. For Scottish folk dancing, attend the Cowal Highland Gathering, which takes place towards the end of August.

Websites of Interest

http://www.visitbritain.com
http://www.myguidebritain.com/
http://wikitravel.org/en/United_Kingdom
http://www.english-heritage.org.uk/
http://www.celticcastles.com/
http://www.tourist-information-uk.com/

Travel Apps

If you are planning to use public transport around the UK, get Journey Pro to help make the best connections.
https://itunes.apple.com/gb/app/journey-pro-london-uk-by-navitime/id388628933

BATH TRAVEL GUIDE

The Around Me app will help you to orient, if you are looking for the nearest ATM, gas station or other convenience services. http://www.aroundmeapp.com/

If you are worried about missing out on a must-see attraction in a particular area, use the National Trust's app to check out the UK's natural and historical treasures. http://www.nationaltrust.org.uk/features/app-privacy-policy

Printed in Great Britain
by Amazon

22864282R00053